Contents

The race is on	2	Destination Egypt	28
Get set for the heat	6	Destination Antarctica	36
Get set for the ice	8	Race to the end	42
Ready, steady, pack!	10	Glossary	44
Destination Chile	12	Index	45
Destination China	20	Extreme racing	46

Written by Rob Alcraft

Collins

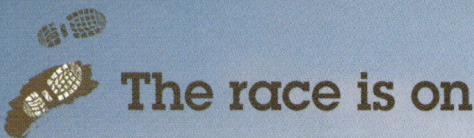

The race is on

The Four Desert Challenge is one of the world's toughest running events. The challenge is four races, across four deserts. Competitors who run all four races must complete a total of 28 days racing. They must run over 1000 kilometres in some of the wildest and loneliest places on Earth.

The four races are held every year, one after the other. Some runners in the Four Desert Challenge are Olympic athletes who compete to win. Athletes like these sometimes run all four races in a single year. Other competitors take longer, running only one race a year. Many compete in teams, helping and encouraging each other when the going gets hard – which it often does!

Each desert race lasts seven days, and is 250 kilometres long.

Each desert race is six stages, run one after the other over seven days. Most stages are 40 kilometres – about the same distance as a marathon. There's a set time to finish each stage, but it's long enough so that competitors don't have to run the whole way – walking is allowed!

Each race also has a stage called the Long March, which is over 80 kilometres. This is the toughest part of every race, and is included to really push racers to their limits. Often competitors don't finish the Long March until late into the night. Up to 3,500 glow sticks are used to mark the course in the darkness. By day the route is marked out with pink flags, ribbon or chalk paint.

There are checkpoints along the race route where the competitors can get water and medical help if they need it. In every desert race there is a team of doctors who volunteer to look after the competitors. They treat injuries, and lots of blisters!

Runners wear head torches so they can see where they're going.

Get set for the heat

For the first three races, competitors have to be prepared to run in extreme heat. They need to wear the right kit to cope with these conditions.

Good training is important to get competitors through the Desert Challenge. Most racers run about 100 kilometres a week in training.

It's also important to eat well. Food like porridge, brown rice and whole-wheat pasta are healthy and give a racer's body the right kind of energy. Lots of fruit and vegetables also help training. Fat and sugar doesn't help a racer's body – so competitors don't eat burgers and cakes!

In the heat of the desert, even a competitor with good training will sweat a lot. As they sweat they quickly lose important salts and minerals. So during the race many competitors wear special patches that feed energy and minerals into their bodies through their skin.

Get set for the ice

The final race is in Antarctica. Competitors can only take part in this challenge if they have run at least two other desert races already.

Running in Antarctica is very different from other desert races. Here the competitors have to battle with the cold. During the race the temperature can fall as low as – 20°C, so in Antarctica the right clothing is important. Get too cold and a racer's body will stop working properly, and begin to shut down. It becomes hard to think or move properly.

This is called **hypothermia**. Warmth is needed quickly, or hypothermia can kill.

One racer trained for running in Antarctica inside an **ice chamber**. It was a good way to test this runner's body and kit.

Usually racers train in mountains and snow near where they live. Competitors from hot countries have to train as normal – and get used to running on snow when they arrive in Antarctica.

Ready, steady, pack!

In the Four Desert Challenge competitors have to carry everything they need on their back. The only thing they're given during the race is extra water. The rules about what a racer must carry are strict, and each racer's kit is checked before being allowed to start.

Water bottles – competitors must carry a minimum of 2.5 litres of water. They drink around 9 litres of water a day.

Some competitors carry snack pouches of high energy gel-foods to "eat" while running.

Warm clothes and sleeping bags for each night-time stop are needed.

Most competitors' packs weigh around 9 kilograms.

Along with head torches, there's a list of over 30 other bits of kit, which include: a whistle, a knife, a compass, salt tablets, toilet paper and a first-aid kit. The rules are that runners have to carry all this too.

Racers don't need to carry a tent. For the first three races, the race organisers set up camp for the competitors, with tents for them to sleep in at the end of each stage.

Racers who compete in the Antarctic live on board a ship, and share cabins. They have hot meals on board too, so only need to carry snacks to help them keep going in the cold.

When you've got the kit, you're ready to race!

Destination Chile

For the first race competitors travel to Chile, South America. In the north of Chile is a **plateau** called the Atacama Desert.

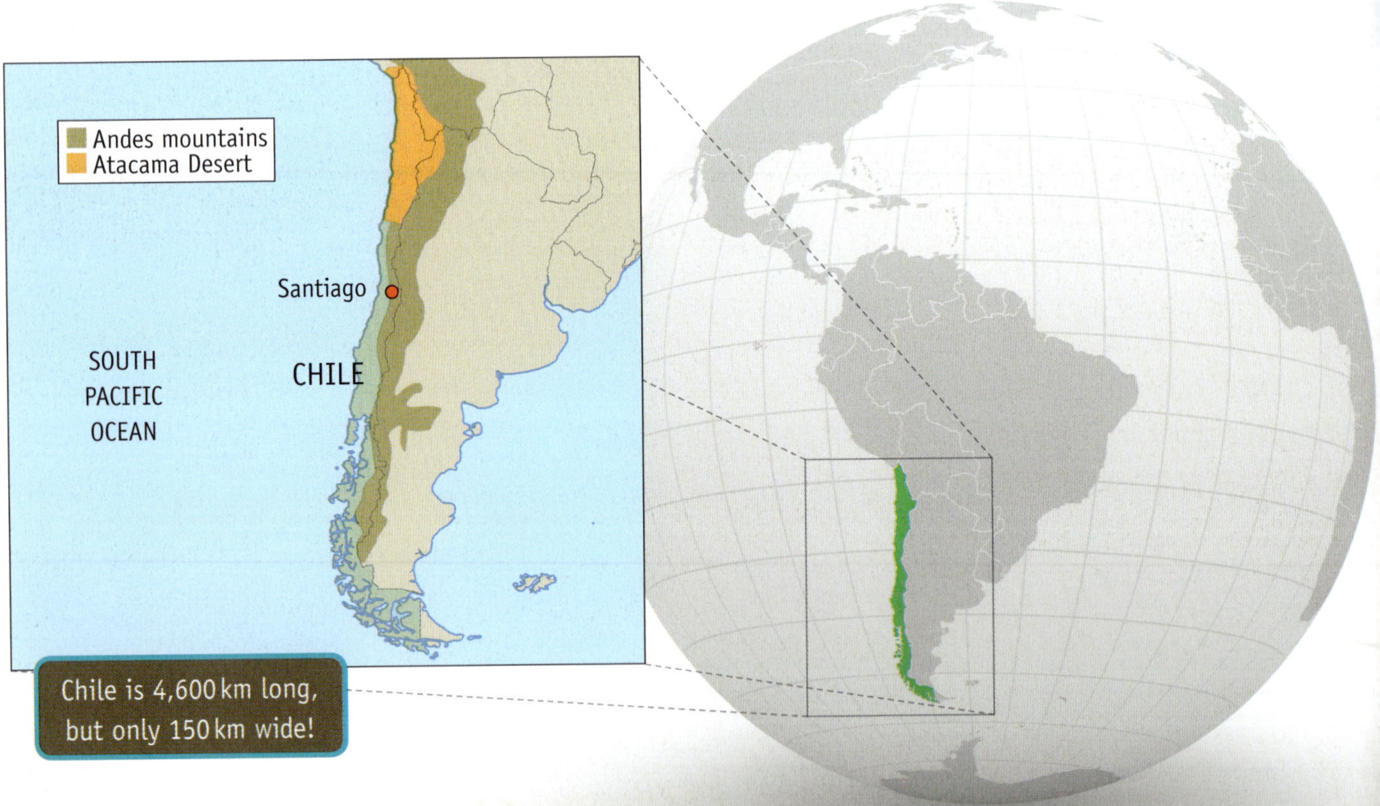

Chile is 4,600 km long, but only 150 km wide!

The Atacama is the driest desert in the world. Some parts of it never have rain. It's so dry and dusty that space scientists even bring robots to the Atacama to test them before sending them to Mars.

👁 Eyewitness

These robots are called "rovers". Rovers have been sent to Mars to collect rock samples and take photographs.

Race 1 – The Atacama Crossing

The Atacama Crossing is a race across rock, **salt flats** and dust. It's hot – the temperature is 40°C. Even so, experienced racers can run this race in about 26 hours. For most competitors, just reaching the finish is enough.

Parts of the Atacama Crossing are over 3,000 metres above sea level. This high up the air is 'thin', which means there is less **oxygen**. Lack of oxygen can cause **mountain sickness**, which is a serious risk for the racers, and makes running harder.

14

👁 Eyewitness

In the very driest parts of the Atacama almost nothing lives. Racers see only the ruins of old mining towns, now quiet and ghostly. They might see bones too! Ancient **mummies** have been found here, buried thousands of years ago by the Chinchorro people, who lived around the desert.

Competitors gather at San Pedro, a small town high up on the edges of the Atacama Desert. Some racers arrive early to get their bodies used to the **altitude**.

Professional athletes are able to finish the first day in less than four hours. But it's hard and rocky and some racers struggle on for more than 10 hours. Reaching the next campsite out in the desert is a welcome chance to rest.

For the next four days competitors **trek** over 160 kilometres, through water-filled canyons, stony valleys and across sand dunes. Then it's the Long March. This is twice the distance of any other stage, and takes competitors into a place called the Valley of the Moon. When night falls many competitors may not have finished. Some sleep at a special checkpoint, others trek through the darkness. The final stage is a short run back into San Pedro.

👁 Eyewitness

The largest animal racers see is the grey desert fox. It eats lizards and insects – and even scorpions. Racers really need to watch out for these, too! The Atacama's red scorpions are only about 4 centimetres long, but they are fast and have a very nasty sting.

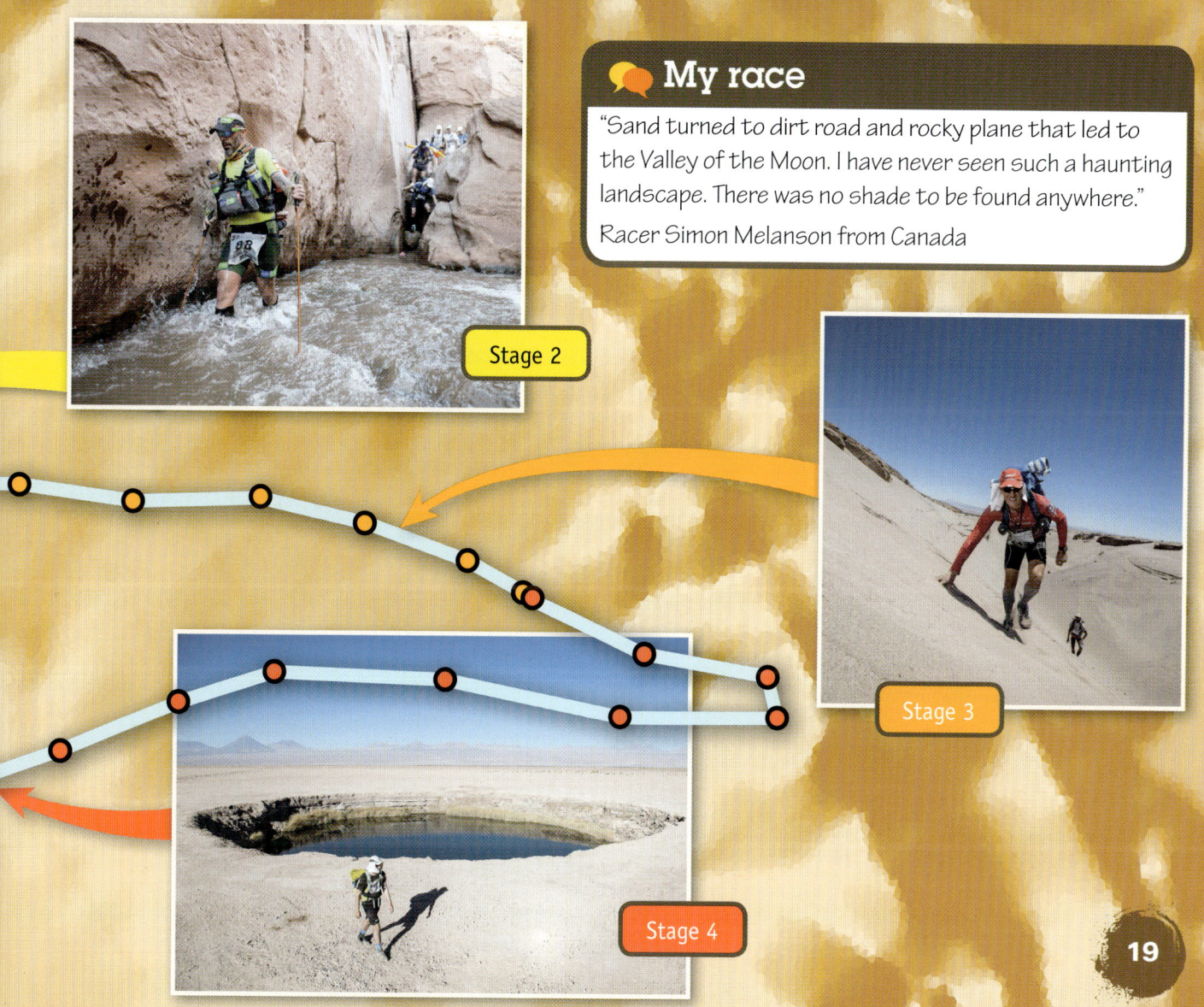

💬 My race

"Sand turned to dirt road and rocky plane that led to the Valley of the Moon. I have never seen such a haunting landscape. There was no shade to be found anywhere."

Racer Simon Melanson from Canada

Stage 2

Stage 3

Stage 4

Destination China

China is one of the world's biggest countries. It has the largest population (over 1.3 billion people!), and many of the world's biggest cities. In the far north is the Gobi Desert. This is the destination for the next desert challenge – the Gobi March.

The Gobi Desert stretches 1,600 kilometres. It's a land of bone-dry plains, sand dunes, mountains and vast grasslands. In the Gobi Desert temperatures are extreme. It gets as cold as −40°C in winter and as hot as 50°C in the summer! Sometimes huge sandstorms sweep over the Gobi Desert, and carry dust across China.

Nomads travel through the Gobi Desert, living in tents called yurts.

Race 2 – The Gobi March

On the Gobi March competitors have to be ready for anything. The race crosses rivers fed by mountain snow, and passes through forests and over steep sand dunes and high cable bridges.

Every mile of the Gobi March is planned by race organisers, with the help of local guides who know the land. The organisers travel ahead of the runners, marking out the course and setting up checkpoints. If rivers swell with mountain rain, or bad weather threatens, they alter the route to make racing possible.

Cable bridges take racers across rivers.

👁 Eyewitness

As they race in the Gobi competitors might just come across a dinosaur! Some of the most important dinosaur **fossils** have been found in the dry rocky parts of the Gobi desert. This is where the world's first dinosaur eggs were discovered.

The first stage of the Gobi March race crosses open, rocky grassland. It's flat, but very hot. Some racers have to drop out with injuries and **exhaustion**.

The next stages take competitors into the Tian Shan mountains, and racers trek up nearly 3,000 metres of sand dunes and mountains. In the evening there are campfires and yurts to sleep in by the Sayram Lake. Then comes the Long March. Experienced racers can complete the stage in just over 8 hours and rest at the next campsite. Others may take over 24 hours to make it to the finish.

> On the Gobi March competitors cross grassy plains and climb mountain slopes.

👁 Eyewitness

Racers find that herds of goats like to visit the campsites. There are two-humped camels in the Gobi Desert too. They can go a month without drinking – and they'll eat almost anything, even old bones!

Stage 5

 My race

"We crossed raging streams over swinging rope bridges, then through forest, before a staggering climb to the highest point of the race."

Racer Steven Brydon from Australia

Finish

Stage 6

27

Destination Egypt

Egypt has one great river flowing through it – the Nile. Almost all of Egypt's people live along the Nile. Beyond the river is a huge, sandy desert where in some places years go by with no rain at all. This is the Sahara, the destination for the third desert challenge.

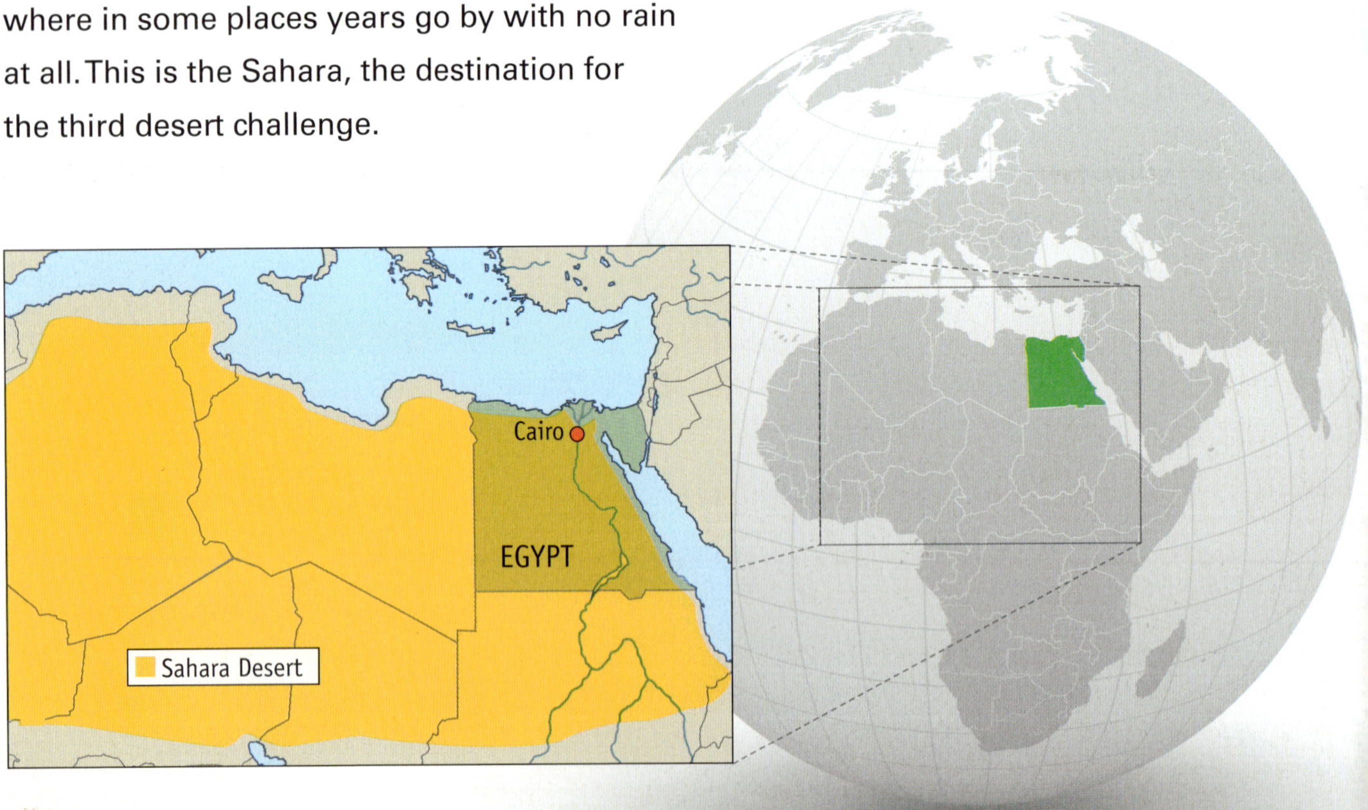

The Sahara is a land of dust, rock and sand dunes that covers almost all of northern Africa. It's the world's hottest desert. In ancient times people used camels to carry goods across the Sahara to trade. Camels are still one of the best ways to travel in the desert.

Large parts of the Sahara are sand and dunes – but there are mountains too.

Race 3 – The Sahara Race

The Sahara Race is across 250 kilometres of dunes and gravel. Running on the sand is hard and temperatures rise close to 50°C.

Drinking water at each checkpoint in the race is important; racers can lose 2 litres of water in sweat in a single hour! Racers have to take care they don't get too hot or thirsty, or they can suffer cramp and **heatstroke**.

👁 Eyewitness

The Sahara has not always been so dry. Among the dunes, racers cross what was once a lake. They pass the fossil bones of whale-like creatures that used to live where there is now dry desert. Deeper into the Sahara there are ancient rock drawings that show cattle and giraffe – and even people swimming.

The race begins in the cool of the early morning near a place known as the Valley of the Whales. There's sand all around, but racers discover that it's not all the same. Sometimes it's packed hard, and perfect for running. At other times the sand is soft and every step is exhausting because your feet sink into it.

The Long March stage is hard. The only shade is at each checkpoint, and when the sun sets at 6.30 p.m. the cool of darkness is a relief. For those who are still racing, the star-filled night is one of the highlights of the race. Some racers trek for over 30 hours on this stage – but they're nearly home. The final stage is just 10 kilometres, and after six days in the sand and heat, racers reach the finish at Egypt's great pyramids.

👁 Eyewitness

For the racers the desert looks empty, but the sand hides ruins and burials from Egypt's past. Whole towns are still being discovered and even pyramids and temples from the time of the **pharaohs**, all hidden from the world under the desert's shifting sands.

The Sahara Race... Go!

Start: Farafra Oasis

Stage 3

Stage 1

Stage 2

34

Stage 4

 My race

"Dunes, sand and more sand with a couple of hills to help!"

Racer Ben Atkin from Britain

Finish: the pyramids, Giza

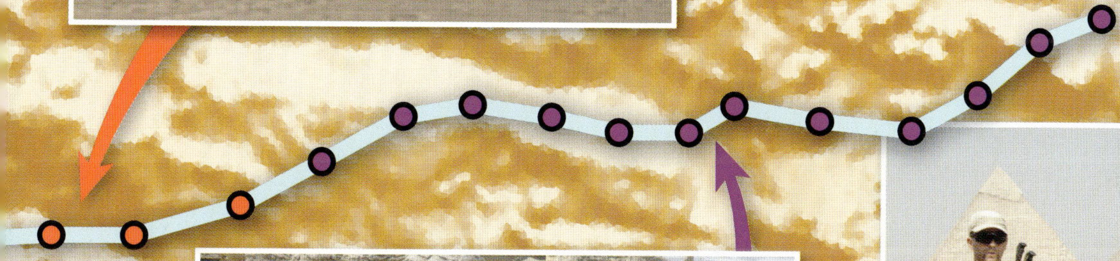

Stage 6

Stage 5

35

Destination Antarctica

This is the final desert challenge – Antarctica. This mountain-filled wilderness is the world's largest desert. In the middle of Antarctica less rain or snow falls than in the Sahara.

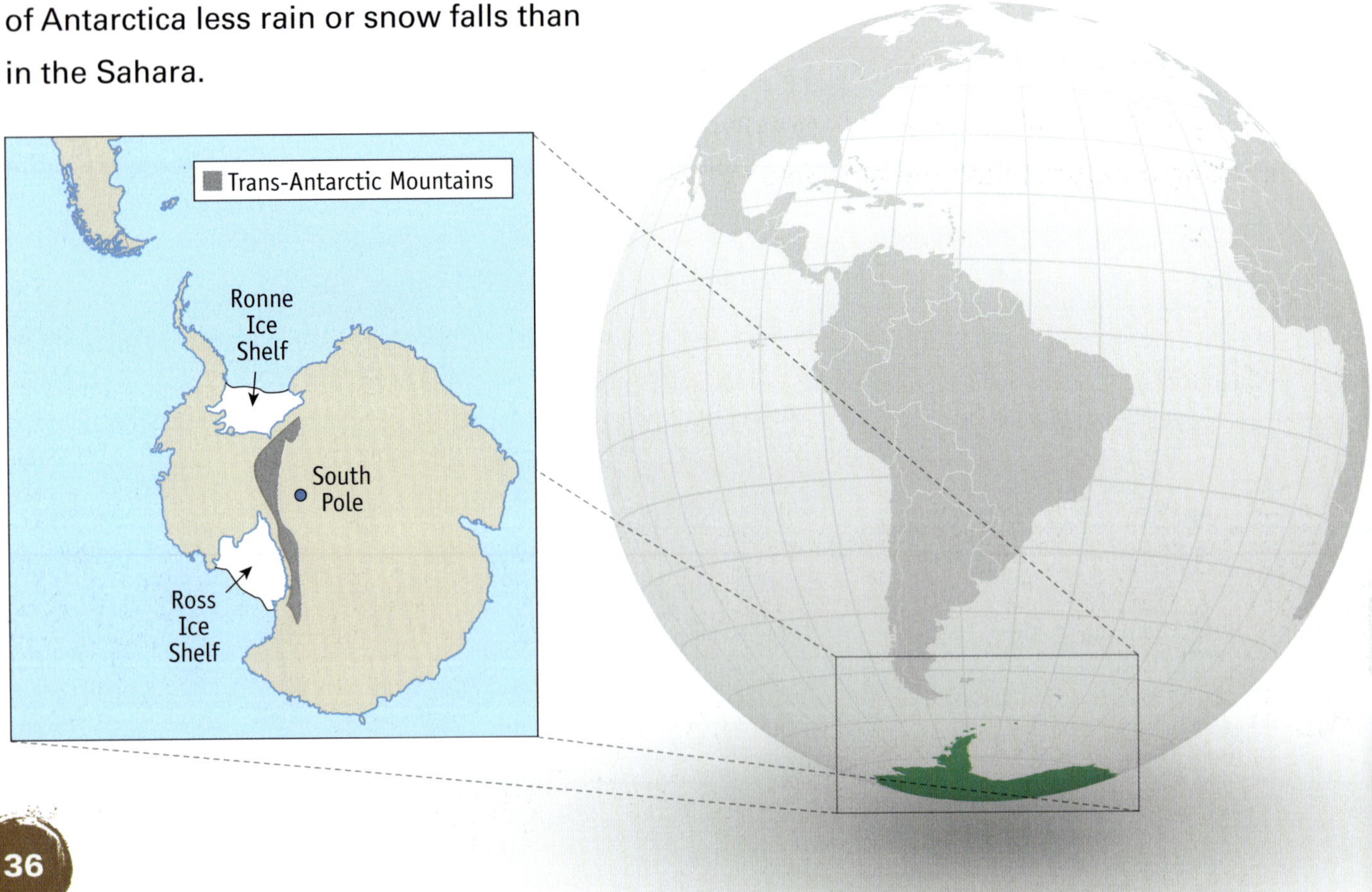

Most of Antarctica is covered in thick sheets of ice. Some of it is over four kilometres deep. This deep ice is very old, falling as snow around 1.5 million years ago. No one lives in Antarctica. There are only scientists who visit and stay in research bases. They come to study the ice and weather, and the amazing creatures that live and feed in the icy seas.

Antarctica is the coldest place on Earth.

Race 4 – The Last Desert

Racers in the Last Desert gather at Ushuaia in Argentina. They travel to the northern tip of Antarctica by ship. The journey takes them across the Drake Passage, and some of the roughest seas in the world.

During the race competitors live on board the ship. Each day they travel to where the wind and weather make racing possible. Open boats ferry competitors from the ship to land.

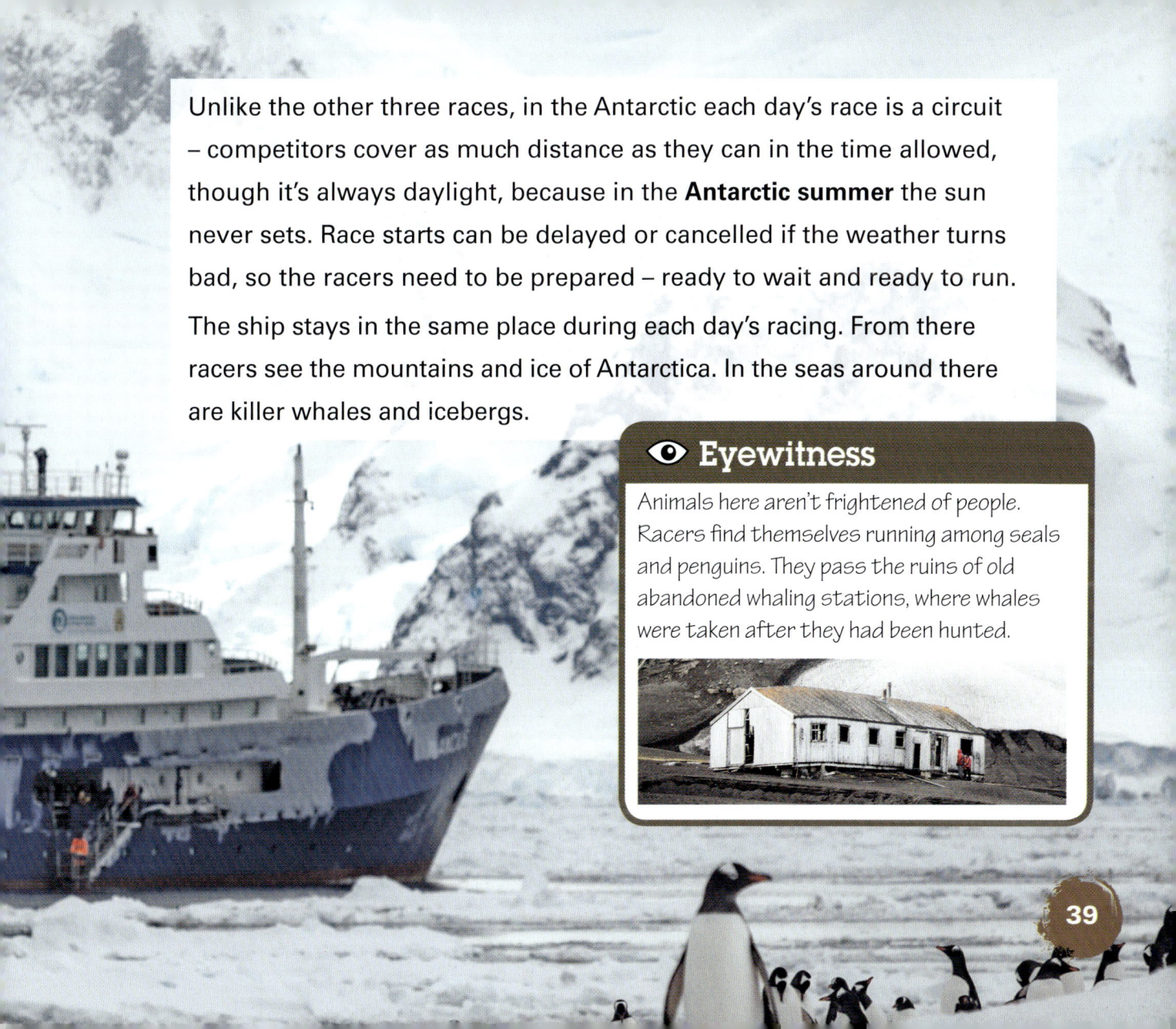

Unlike the other three races, in the Antarctic each day's race is a circuit – competitors cover as much distance as they can in the time allowed, though it's always daylight, because in the **Antarctic summer** the sun never sets. Race starts can be delayed or cancelled if the weather turns bad, so the racers need to be prepared – ready to wait and ready to run.

The ship stays in the same place during each day's racing. From there racers see the mountains and ice of Antarctica. In the seas around there are killer whales and icebergs.

👁 Eyewitness

Animals here aren't frightened of people. Racers find themselves running among seals and penguins. They pass the ruins of old abandoned whaling stations, where whales were taken after they had been hunted.

The Last Desert… Go!

Stage 2

Stage 3

Stage 5

40

Finish: Telefon Bay, Deception Island

Start: Deception Island

Stage 1

Stage 4 – cancelled because of a storm

💬 My race

"Beautiful mountains, shimmering blue water and all of the penguins you could ever hope for."

Racer Shane Stoik from Canada

Race to the end

Competitors who have completed all four desert races have trekked 1,000 kilometres. They've been to the driest, hottest and coldest places on Earth. These racers have tested themselves to their limit, and it is an experience that they'll never forget.

Many write **blogs** and post videos describing their experiences of running in these deserts, and how good it feels to finish. Racers receive medals, but the real prize is taking on the challenge – and reaching the end. Many racers also find that those they have run with are their friends for life.

> A small number of racers have completed all 1,000 km of the Four Desert Challenge in just one year – the Desert Grand Slam.

💬 **My race**

"First people have to dream, and then everything is possible."

Racer Beatriz Camiade from Mexico

43

Glossary

Antarctic summer	when the southern half of the world is closest to the sun, and Antarctica has its summer and 24 hour daylight
altitude	the height above sea level
blogs	personal online journals
exhaustion	extreme tiredness
fossils	remains of animals or plants that lived millions of years ago
frostbite	damage to parts of the body caused by freezing
heatstroke	fever due to spending too long in extreme heat
hypothermia	dangerously low body temperature
ice chamber	a specially cooled room
mountain sickness	sickness, headache and shortness of breath caused by high altitude
mummies	bodies preserved for burial
oxygen	a gas found in air
pharaohs	Ancient Egyptian kings
plateau	wide, flat area of high land
salt flats	areas of salt left after large amounts of water have completely evaporated
trek	a long, difficult journey made on foot

Index

Antarctica 8, 36, 37, 38, 39

Atacama Crossing, the 14, 18, 19

Atacama Desert, the 12, 13, 16

Chile 12, 13

China 20, 21, 26, 27

cold 8, 9, 11, 21, 37, 42

desert 2, 3, 4, 5, 6, 7, 8, 10, 12, 13, 15, 16, 17, 20, 21, 23, 25, 28, 29, 31, 33, 36, 38, 40, 42

Desert Grand Slam 42

Egypt 28, 32, 33

Gobi Desert, the 20, 21

Gobi March, the 20, 21, 23, 25

grasslands 21 21

heat 6, 30, 32

ice 8, 9, 36, 37, 39

Last Desert 38, 40

Long March 5, 17, 24, 32

mountains 8, 12, 20, 21, 24, 29, 36, 39, 41

Sahara Desert, the 28, 29

Sahara Race 30, 34, 35

training 6, 8

Extreme racing

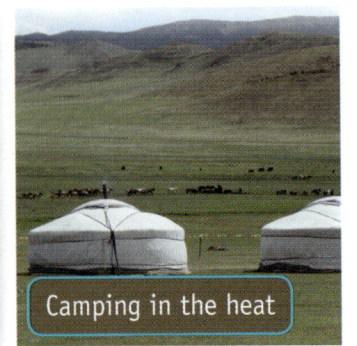

Mountain racing

Wet

Night time racing

Flat racing

Camping in the heat

46

Camping in the cold

Cold

Hot

Dry

47

Ideas for reading

Written by Clare Dowdall, PhD
Lecturer and Primary Literacy Consultant

Reading objectives/requirements:
- read for a range of purposes
- ask questions to improve understanding
- make predictions from details stated and implied
- retrieve and record information from non-fiction

Spoken language objectives/requirements:
- use spoken language to develop understanding through speculating, hypothesizing, imagining and exploring ideas

Curriculum links: Geography – locational knowledge

Resources: ICT for research, pens and paper

Build a context for reading

- Look at the front cover and discuss what is happening. Ask children to suggest what the Four Desert Challenge will involve.
- Read the blurb aloud and compare the information to the children's ideas. Check that they understand what "ultimate endurance" event means.
- Ask children to describe what they know about deserts. Can they name any famous deserts? Do they know where any deserts are?

Understand and apply reading strategies

- Ask children to read to p5. and then recount some of the key information about the Four Desert challenge. Model how to find important facts when reading and make a note of them on a whiteboard, using a list, or spider diagram.
- Develop their understanding and prepare for further reading by asking children to imagine what it would be like to spend seven days in the desert, racing and camping in a tent. What would they find hard? Would they like the challenge?